I0479292

Google for Business

This a simple guide to mostly free but, some paid tools created by Google to help you grow your business.

This book won't solve all your Google problems, but it will give you a headstart.

Compiled By:

Trey Carmichael
Stephen Swanson

Table of Contents

Introduction

In today's fast-paced digital world, businesses are constantly seeking new ways to thrive and stay ahead of the competition. The internet has democratized access to resources, allowing businesses to harness a wealth of tools to grow, innovate, and succeed. One such powerhouse of digital resources is Google, a name synonymous with online innovation, search, and countless other services. But did you know that Google offers a plethora of tools specifically designed to help businesses excel in the digital landscape? Welcome to "Google For Business," the ultimate guide to leveraging Google's extensive suite of tools and resources to propel your business to new heights.

In this book, we will delve into the diverse range of Google's offerings tailored for businesses, from local shops to multinational corporations, nonprofits to online retailers. As we explore each tool, you'll learn how to get started, optimize their features, and harness their capabilities to elevate your business operations.

Our journey begins with Google My Business, a powerful platform to enhance your online presence and connect with local customers. We'll then guide you through Google Workspace, an all-in-one collaboration and productivity suite designed to streamline your business processes.

We'll also delve into YouTube, the world's second-largest search engine, and show you how to make the most of its potential for your marketing and content creation needs. Our tour will continue through the realms of Google Ads, Google Analytics, Google Search Console, and more, equipping you with the knowledge to maximize your visibility, track your success, and make data-driven decisions.

But that's not all! We'll introduce you to Google's specialized tools for retail, nonprofits, and small businesses, ensuring that no matter your niche, you'll find a Google solution to help you flourish. And with resources like Google Alerts, Google Forms, and Google Cloud Platform, you'll have all the information and infrastructure you need to stay informed and agile in an ever-evolving business landscape.

"Google For Business" is your comprehensive roadmap to navigating Google's vast ecosystem of resources, giving you the insights and practical tips you need to make the most of these powerful tools. Whether you're a seasoned entrepreneur, a marketing professional, or a small business owner taking your first steps into the digital world, this book is designed to empower you with the knowledge to harness the full potential of Google for your business success.

So, let's embark on this exciting journey together and unlock the power of Google for your business. Your digital transformation starts here.

Google My Business

1.1 What is Google My Business?

Google My Business (GMB) is a free, easy-to-use tool that allows businesses to manage their online presence across Google Search and Google Maps. With a GMB profile, businesses can showcase essential information such as location, contact details, hours of operation, and customer reviews. By creating and maintaining a GMB profile, businesses can optimize their visibility in local search results, engage with customers, and build trust with potential clients.

1.2 The Importance of a Google My Business Profile

In an increasingly digital world, customers rely on the internet to research and discover local businesses. A GMB profile enables business owners to stand out in local search results, giving them a competitive edge. Here are some key reasons why having a GMB profile is essential for business owners:

1.2.1 Enhanced Local Search Visibility

When users perform a local search (e.g., "coffee shop near me"), Google prioritizes businesses with a GMB profile in its search results. By creating and optimizing your GMB profile, you increase your chances of appearing in the top search results, driving more traffic to your website or physical location.

1.2.2 Google Maps Integration

Google Maps is a go-to resource for users seeking directions, nearby businesses, or local services. By having a GMB profile, your business location will be displayed on Google Maps, making it easy for customers to find and visit your store or office.

1.2.3 Customer Reviews and Ratings

GMB profiles allow customers to leave reviews and ratings, providing social proof of your business's quality and reliability. Positive reviews can attract new customers, while constructive feedback helps you improve your services. Responding to reviews also demonstrates your commitment to customer satisfaction.

1.2.4 Showcase Products and Services

With a GMB profile, you can upload photos, create posts, and highlight special offers, giving potential customers a glimpse of what your business offers. This visual content can help you stand out from competitors and entice customers to choose your business.

1.2.5 Analytics Insights

Google My Business provides analytics data, such as search queries, customer actions, and phone call data, helping you understand how customers find and interact with your business. These insights can guide your marketing strategy and inform your decision-making process.

1.3 How to Set Up and Optimize Your Google My Business Profile

Creating and optimizing a GMB profile is a straightforward process. Follow these steps to get started:

1.3.1 Sign Up and Claim Your Listing

To create a GMB profile, visit the Google My Business website (https://www.google.com/business/) and sign in with your Google account. Click "Manage now" and follow the prompts to add your business details, including name, address, phone number, and category. If your business is already listed, click "Claim this business" to verify ownership.

1.3.2 Verify Your Business

Google requires verification to ensure the accuracy of your business information. Verification can be done through various methods such as postcard, phone, or email. Follow the prompts to complete the verification process.

1.3.3 Optimize Your Profile

Once verified, optimize your GMB profile with the following information:

Business hours: Update your hours of operation, including special hours for holidays or events.

Description: Write a concise, engaging description highlighting your products, services, or unique selling points.

Photos: Upload high-quality photos of your business, products, or services to visually showcase your offerings.

Services: List the services you provide, adding descriptions and pricing when applicable.

Attributes: Select relevant attributes (e.g., "Wheelchair accessible") to provide additional information about your business.

1.3.4 Manage Customer Reviews

Encourage satisfied customers to leave reviews on your GMB profile and monitor incoming reviews regularly. Respond to both positive and negative feedback in a professional, timely manner. Addressing concerns demonstrates your commitment to customer satisfaction, while expressing gratitude for positive reviews fosters customer loyalty.

1.3.5 Create Google Posts

Google Posts allow you to share updates, events, promotions, or announcements directly on your GMB profile. Regularly creating relevant, engaging posts keeps your profile fresh and provides additional value to potential customers.

1.3.6 Use Google My Business Messaging

GMB Messaging enables customers to send direct messages to your business through your GMB profile. Activate this feature to improve customer engagement and answer inquiries in real-time.

1.4 Leveraging Google My Business for Success

With a fully optimized GMB profile, you'll be well on your way to boosting your online presence and driving more customers to your business. To maximize the benefits of GMB, consider the following best practices:

1.4.1 Keep Your Information Up-to-Date

Regularly review your GMB profile to ensure all information is accurate and up-to-date.

Changes in business hours, contact details, or services can impact customer experience, so it's crucial to maintain an accurate profile.

1.4.2 Monitor and Respond to Questions

Customers can ask questions on your GMB profile, providing an opportunity to address concerns and demonstrate your expertise. Monitor and respond to questions promptly to build trust and credibility with potential clients.

1.4.3 Analyze Insights and Adjust Your Strategy

Review your GMB analytics data to understand customer behavior and identify trends. Use this information to refine your marketing strategy, optimize your profile, or improve your products and services.

1.4.4 Encourage Customer-Generated Content

Ask satisfied customers to leave reviews or share photos of their experience with your business. User-generated content can boost your online reputation and create a sense of community around your brand.

1.4.5 Integrate GMB with Other Google Tools

Leverage the full power of Google by integrating your GMB profile with other Google tools like Google Ads, Google Analytics, and Google Search Console. Combining these resources can provide a comprehensive view of your online presence and help you optimize your overall digital marketing strategy.

In conclusion, Google My Business is an essential tool for businesses looking to enhance their online presence, engage with customers, and attract new clients. By creating, verifying, and optimizing your GMB profile, you can take advantage of the numerous benefits this platform offers. By following the best practices outlined in this chapter, you'll be well on your way to harnessing the power of Google My Business for your success.

TL ; DR

Google My Business (GMB) is a free tool that allows businesses to manage their online presence across Google Search and Google Maps. A GMB profile is essential for enhancing local search visibility, showcasing products and services, and engaging with customers through reviews, questions, and messaging. To optimize your GMB profile, sign up, verify your business, and provide accurate, up-to-date information. Leverage GMB insights to refine your marketing strategy and integrate GMB with other Google tools to maximize your online success.

Google Sites

15.1 What are Google Sites?

Google Sites is a free, user-friendly website builder that allows users to create and manage websites without the need for extensive coding or web design experience. With its intuitive drag-and-drop interface, Google Sites enables business owners to create professional-looking websites to showcase their products or services, share information, and engage with their customers.

15.2 Why are Google Sites Important for Business Owners?

Google Sites offer several benefits for business owners, including:

15.2.1 Ease of Use

With its simple interface and drag-and-drop functionality, Google Sites allows users with little or no web design experience to create and maintain websites.

15.2.2 Cost Efficiency

Google Sites is a free service, making it an ideal solution for small businesses or startups looking to establish an online presence without incurring significant costs.

15.2.3 Integration with Google Workspace

Google Sites seamlessly integrates with other Google Workspace tools, such as Google Drive, Calendar, and Google Analytics, allowing you to easily incorporate these services into your website.

15.2.4 Collaboration

Multiple users can work on a Google Site simultaneously, making it easy for teams to collaborate on website design and content updates.

15.3 How to Get Started with Google Sites

To create a website using Google Sites, follow these steps:

15.3.1 Access Google Sites

Visit the Google Sites website (https://sites.google.com/) and sign in with your Google account.

15.3.2 Choose a Template or Start from Scratch

Once signed in, you can choose from a variety of pre-designed templates or start with a blank canvas. Select the option that best suits your needs and click "Create."

15.3.3 Customize Your Site

Use the drag-and-drop interface to add elements such as text, images, videos, and links to your site. Customize the site's appearance by changing fonts, colors, and layout options.

15.3.4 Add Pages and Navigation

Create additional pages for your site by clicking the "Add Page" button. Organize your pages using the built-in navigation features, such as menus and sidebars.

15.3.5 Integrate Google Workspace Tools

Incorporate other Google Workspace services, such as Google Drive, Calendar, and Maps, into your site by adding the corresponding widgets.

15.3.6 Preview and Publish Your Site

Click the "Preview" button to see how your site will appear to visitors. When you're satisfied with your design, click "Publish" to make your site live.

15.3.7 Share Your Site

Share your site's URL with your customers, include it in your email signature, or add it to your social media profiles to increase visibility and attract visitors.

15.4 Tips for Creating Effective Google Sites

To ensure your Google Site is engaging and effective, consider the following best practices:

15.4.1 Plan Your Site's Structure

Before you start building your site, create a plan for its structure, including the pages you'll need and how they'll be organized.

15.4.2 Keep Your Design Simple and Professional

Choose a clean, professional design for your site, and avoid cluttering it with too many elements or distractions.

15.4.3 Make Your Site Mobile-Friendly

Ensure your site looks good and functions well on mobile devices, as many users will access your site from their smartphones or tablets.

15.4.4 Use High-Quality Images and Multimedia

Incorporate high-quality images and multimedia elements that showcase your products or services and enhance your site's visual appeal.

15.4.5 Update Your Site Regularly

Keep your site up to date with the latest information about your business, products, services, and promotions to keep your visitors engaged and informed.

15.4.6 Optimize Your Site for SEO

Use search engine optimization (SEO) best practices, such as incorporating relevant keywords and optimizing meta tags, to improve your site's visibility in search engine results.

15.4.7 Test and Refine Your Site

Regularly test your site's performance, usability, and appearance on different devices and browsers. Make improvements and refinements based on your findings and user feedback.

15.4.8 Monitor Your Site's Analytics

Use Google Analytics to track your site's traffic, user behavior, and engagement, allowing you to make data-driven decisions and improvements.

15.4.9 Encourage Visitor Engagement

Include calls to action (CTAs) and interactive elements, such as contact forms and social media buttons, to encourage visitors to engage with your business.

In conclusion, Google Sites is a user-friendly and cost-effective solution for business owners looking to create professional websites without the need for extensive coding or web design experience. By following the steps to get started with Google Sites and implementing best practices, you can create an engaging and effective website that showcases your products or services, shares information, and connects with your customers.

TL ; DR

Google Sites is a free, user-friendly website builder that allows business owners to create professional-looking websites without extensive coding or web design experience. It offers ease of use, cost efficiency, integration with Google Workspace, and collaboration features. To get started, access Google Sites, choose a template or start from scratch, customize your site, add pages and navigation, integrate Google Workspace tools, preview, publish, and share your site. To create an effective website, plan its structure, keep the design simple, make it mobile-friendly, use high-quality images, update regularly, optimize for SEO, test and refine, monitor analytics, and encourage visitor engagement.

Google Workspace (formerly G Suite)

2.1 What is Google Workspace?

Google Workspace, formerly known as G Suite, is a collection of cloud-based productivity and collaboration tools designed for businesses. With Google Workspace, organizations can access essential applications like Gmail, Google Drive, Google Calendar, Google Docs, Google Sheets, Google Slides, Google Meet, and more, all within a single platform. These applications enable seamless collaboration, real-time editing, and secure file storage, allowing businesses to streamline their operations and work efficiently.

2.2 The Importance of Google Workspace for Business Owners

In today's fast-paced and increasingly remote work environment, having a suite of reliable, user-friendly, and secure tools is essential for any business owner. Google Workspace offers a range of benefits, including:

2.2.1 Improved Collaboration

Google Workspace facilitates collaboration by allowing multiple users to access and edit documents, spreadsheets, and presentations in real-time. This feature reduces the need for email attachments, version tracking, and time-consuming back-and-forth communication.

2.2.2 Centralized File Storage

Google Drive, the cloud storage solution within Google Workspace, enables secure storage and easy access to files from any device with an internet connection. Centralized storage simplifies file organization and eliminates the risk of data loss due to hardware failure.

2.2.3 Integrated Communication Tools

Google Workspace includes Gmail, Google Meet, and Google Chat, allowing teams to communicate seamlessly through email, video conferencing, and instant messaging. These integrated tools foster efficient communication and collaboration within organizations.

2.2.4 Enhanced Security and Compliance

Google Workspace offers advanced security features such as two-factor authentication, data encryption, and customizable access controls, ensuring your business data remains protected. Additionally, Google Workspace complies with various industry regulations, including GDPR and HIPAA.

2.2.5 Scalability and Flexibility

Google Workspace offers various pricing plans to accommodate businesses of all sizes. As your business grows, you can easily scale your Google Workspace subscription to meet your needs, adding or removing users as required.

2.3 How to Get Started with Google Workspace

Setting up Google Workspace for your business is a straightforward process. Follow these steps to get started:

2.3.1 Sign Up for Google Workspace

Visit the Google Workspace website (https://workspace.google.com/) and click "Get Started" to begin the signup process. Choose a pricing plan that best suits your business needs and enter your business information, including your domain name. If you don't have a domain, you can purchase one through Google during the signup process.

2.3.2 Create Your Admin Account

During signup, you'll be prompted to create an administrator account for your Google Workspace subscription. This account will have full access to manage users, billing, and settings for your organization.

2.3.3 Add Users to Your Google Workspace Account

Once your admin account is set up, you can add users to your Google Workspace subscription. In the admin console, navigate to "Users," click "Add new user," and enter the user's name and email address. Repeat this process for each team member you want to add.

2.3.4 Set Up Email with Google Workspace

Google Workspace includes Gmail for your custom domain (e.g., user@yourdomain.com). To configure your email, access the admin console, and navigate to "Apps" > "Google Workspace" > "Gmail." Follow the prompts to set up email routing and verify your domain.

2.3.5 Explore and Customize Google Workspace Apps

Familiarize yourself with the Google Workspace applications, such as Google Drive, Google Docs, and Google Meet. Customize the settings for each app to meet your organization's needs, and provide your team with the necessary access permissions.

2.3.6 Train Your Team on Google Workspace

To maximize the benefits of Google Workspace, ensure your team is familiar with the platform and its applications. Provide training resources, such as Google's own tutorials, or consider third-party training programs to help your employees become proficient in using Google Workspace tools.

2.3.7 Configure Security Settings

Google Workspace offers various security features to protect your organization's data. In the admin console, navigate to "Security" and configure settings such as two-factor authentication, password requirements, and access controls.

2.4 Tips for Maximizing Google Workspace Efficiency

To make the most of your Google Workspace subscription, consider these best practices:

2.4.1 Create a Shared Team Drive

A shared Team Drive in Google Drive allows you to centralize files and resources for your entire team. This feature simplifies file management, streamlines collaboration, and ensures that important documents are accessible to all relevant team members.

2.4.2 Leverage Google Workspace Add-Ons

There are numerous add-ons available for Google Workspace applications, such as project management tools, CRM integrations, and document signing services. Explore the available add-ons to enhance the functionality of your Google Workspace tools and customize them to your business needs.

2.4.3 Utilize Google Workspace Templates

Google Docs, Sheets, and Slides offer various templates for common business documents, such as reports, invoices, and meeting agendas. Utilize these templates to save time and maintain consistent formatting across your organization.

2.4.4 Schedule Regular Google Meet Video Conferences

Regular video conferences via Google Meet can improve team communication, foster collaboration, and keep remote employees engaged. Schedule routine meetings to ensure your team stays connected and aligned.

2.4.5 Integrate Google Workspace with Other Business Tools

Many business tools, such as project management platforms, CRM systems, and accounting software, offer integrations with Google Workspace. Leverage these integrations to streamline your business processes and create a cohesive digital ecosystem.

In conclusion, Google Workspace is a powerful suite of productivity and collaboration tools that can help businesses operate more efficiently, improve communication, and enhance security. By following the steps outlined in this chapter, you can set up and customize Google Workspace to meet your organization's unique needs. Embracing best practices and leveraging integrations will enable you to maximize the potential of Google Workspace and drive your business to success.

TL ; DR

Google Workspace is a suite of cloud-based productivity and collaboration tools designed for businesses, including Gmail, Google Drive, Google Calendar, Google Docs, and more. These tools enable seamless collaboration, real-time editing, secure file storage, and integrated communication. To set up Google Workspace, sign up, create an admin account, add users, configure email, and explore the available apps. Maximize efficiency by creating a shared Team Drive, leveraging add-ons, utilizing templates, scheduling regular Google Meet conferences, and integrating with other business tools.

YouTube

3.1 What is YouTube?

YouTube is the world's largest video-sharing platform, allowing users to upload, view, and share videos on a wide range of topics. Owned by Google, YouTube has become a powerful marketing tool for businesses looking to reach and engage with their target audience through video content. With over 2 billion monthly active users and an increasingly influential role in the consumer decision-making process, YouTube presents a significant opportunity for business owners to expand their reach and grow their brand.

3.2 The Importance of YouTube for Business Owners

In the current digital landscape, video content is king. YouTube offers various benefits for business owners, including:

3.2.1 Increased Brand Visibility

With its massive user base and robust search capabilities, YouTube provides a platform for businesses to reach a broad audience and increase brand exposure.

3.2.2 Enhanced Customer Engagement

Video content is more engaging and shareable than text-based content, allowing businesses to capture their audience's attention and foster meaningful interactions.

3.2.3 Improved SEO

As a Google-owned platform, YouTube videos are indexed in Google search results, contributing to your overall search engine optimization (SEO) efforts and driving traffic to your website.

3.2.4 Cost-Effective Marketing

YouTube offers a cost-effective way to create and distribute marketing content, with the potential for significant returns on investment as videos gain traction and reach a wider audience.

3.2.5 Versatility

YouTube allows businesses to create various types of video content, such as product demos, how-to tutorials, customer testimonials, and behind-the-scenes footage, catering to diverse marketing objectives and audience preferences.

3.3 How to Get Started with YouTube

To begin leveraging YouTube for your business, follow these steps:

3.3.1 Create a YouTube Channel

First, sign in to YouTube with your Google account. Click your profile icon in the top right corner and select "Create a channel." Choose "Use a custom name" to create a channel with your business name, and follow the prompts to complete the setup process.

3.3.2 Optimize Your Channel

Customize your YouTube channel to reflect your brand identity and provide relevant information about your business. Include the following elements:

Channel art: Design an eye-catching banner that represents your brand.
Profile picture: Upload your business logo or an image that accurately represents your brand.
Channel description: Write a compelling description that highlights your business's mission and the type of content viewers can expect.
Contact information: Include your website URL, email address, and social media links.

3.3.3 Plan Your Video Content

Develop a content strategy that aligns with your marketing objectives and caters to your target audience's preferences. Consider creating a content calendar to plan and schedule your video uploads.

3.3.4 Produce High-Quality Videos

Invest in quality video production, including proper lighting, sound, and editing. While you don't need a large budget or professional equipment, ensure your videos are polished and visually appealing to engage your audience.

3.3.5 Optimize Your Video Metadata

When uploading a video, optimize its metadata to improve its visibility in search results. Include:

A descriptive, keyword-rich title
A compelling thumbnail image
A detailed video description, including relevant keywords and links
Relevant video tags to help YouTube understand your content
3.3.6 Promote Your Videos

Share your YouTube videos on your website, blog, and social media channels to maximize their reach. Encourage viewers to like, comment, and subscribe to your channel, as these interactions contribute to your video's visibility.

3.3.7 Monitor and Analyze Your Channel Performance

Use YouTube Analytics to track your channel's performance, including view counts, watch time, audience demographics, and engagement metrics. Analyze this data to identify trends, uncover content preferences, and refine your video marketing strategy.

3.4 Tips for YouTube Success

To maximize the potential of your YouTube channel, consider these best practices:

3.4.1 Consistency is Key

Upload videos regularly to keep your audience engaged and build a loyal subscriber base. Maintain a consistent theme, style, and tone across your videos to create a cohesive brand identity.

3.4.2 Engage with Your Audience

Encourage viewers to leave comments and respond to their feedback, fostering a sense of community and building relationships with your audience. Use the Community tab to share updates, polls, and behind-the-scenes content to maintain engagement between video uploads.

3.4.3 Collaborate with Other Creators

Partner with other YouTube creators in your niche or industry to create collaborative content, tapping into each other's audiences and increasing your overall reach.

3.4.4 Leverage YouTube Advertising

Consider using YouTube advertising options, such as TrueView, bumper ads, or sponsored cards, to promote your videos, drive traffic to your website, or generate leads.

3.4.5 Optimize Your Videos for Mobile

With a growing number of users accessing YouTube via mobile devices, ensure your videos are optimized for mobile viewing, including text readability, video format, and load times.

3.4.6 Explore YouTube Features

Stay up-to-date with YouTube's latest features and tools, such as YouTube Shorts, YouTube Stories, and YouTube Live, to diversify your content and stay ahead of the competition.

In conclusion, YouTube presents a significant opportunity for business owners to reach and engage with their target audience through the power of video marketing. By creating a YouTube channel, optimizing your content, and employing best practices, you can harness the platform's potential to increase brand visibility, drive website traffic, and grow your business.

TL ; DR

YouTube is the world's largest video-sharing platform, offering businesses a powerful marketing tool to reach and engage with their target audience through video content. To leverage YouTube, create a channel, optimize it with your branding, plan and produce high-quality videos, optimize video metadata, promote your content, and monitor performance using YouTube Analytics. Maximize success by maintaining consistency, engaging with your audience, collaborating with other creators, leveraging YouTube advertising, optimizing for mobile, and exploring YouTube features.

Google Ads

4.1 What are Google Ads?

Google Ads is a powerful online advertising platform that allows businesses to create and display targeted ads on Google Search, Google Display Network, and YouTube. Using a pay-per-click (PPC) model, advertisers only pay when users click on their ads. Google Ads offers a variety of ad formats, such as text-based search ads, display ads with images or videos, and shopping ads that showcase products. With advanced targeting and bidding options, businesses can optimize their ad campaigns to reach their target audience effectively and maximize their return on investment (ROI).

4.2 The Importance of Google Ads for Business Owners

Google Ads presents numerous benefits for business owners, including:

4.2.1 Increased Online Visibility

By placing your ads in prominent positions on Google Search results and the Google Display Network, you can boost your online visibility and reach a wider audience.

4.2.2 Targeted Advertising

Google Ads enables precise targeting based on keywords, demographics, location, interests, and more, ensuring that your ads are displayed to the right audience at the right time.

4.2.3 Measurable Results

Google Ads provides detailed analytics and tracking tools, allowing you to monitor your campaign performance, measure your ROI, and optimize your advertising strategy.

4.2.4 Budget Control

With Google Ads, you set your daily budget and maximum bid per click, giving you full control over your advertising expenses.

4.2.5 Flexibility

Google Ads offers various ad formats, targeting options, and bidding strategies, allowing you to customize your campaigns to suit your unique business objectives and marketing goals.

4.3 How to Get Started with Google Ads

To launch your first Google Ads campaign, follow these steps:

4.3.1 Create a Google Ads Account

Visit the Google Ads website (https://ads.google.com/) and sign in with your Google account. If you don't have an account, create one by following the prompts.

4.3.2 Set Up Your First Campaign

Click "New Campaign" and choose your campaign goal, such as increasing website traffic, generating leads, or driving sales. Select the campaign type (Search, Display, Shopping, Video, or Smart), set your budget and bidding strategy, and configure your targeting options.

4.3.3 Create Your Ad Groups

Ad groups allow you to organize your ads based on similar themes or keywords. Create one or more ad groups, each targeting a specific set of keywords or audience.

4.3.4 Write Your Ad Copy

Craft compelling ad copy that clearly communicates your value proposition and includes a strong call-to-action (CTA). Be sure to incorporate relevant keywords to improve your ad relevancy and quality score.

4.3.5 Add Ad Extensions

Ad extensions enhance your ads with additional information, such as phone numbers, location, or site links. Utilize relevant ad extensions to improve your ad's visibility and click-through rate (CTR).

4.3.6 Launch Your Campaign

Once your ads and ad groups are set up, review your campaign settings, and click "Publish" to launch your campaign.

4.3.7 Monitor and Optimize Your Campaign Performance

Use Google Ads' performance metrics and reporting tools to track your campaign's success. Analyze the data to identify areas for improvement, such as adjusting your bidding strategy, refining your targeting, or testing new ad copy.

4.4 Tips for Google Ads Success

To maximize the potential of your Google Ads campaigns, consider these best practices:

4.4.1 Conduct Thorough Keyword Research

Identify relevant, high-converting keywords for your campaigns using tools like Google Keyword Planner, and group them into tightly-themed ad groups.

4.4.2 Focus on Ad Quality

Aim to achieve a high Quality Score by creating relevant and engaging ads that match the intent of your target keywords. A higher Quality Score can lead to lower costs per click (CPC) and better ad positions.

4.4.3 Use Negative Keywords

Negative keywords prevent your ads from showing for irrelevant search queries, saving you money on wasted clicks and improving your overall campaign performance.

4.4.4 Test and Refine Your Ad Copy

Experiment with different headlines, descriptions, and CTAs to determine which combinations resonate best with your target audience. Regularly review and update your ad copy to optimize your CTR and conversion rates.

4.4.5 Implement Conversion Tracking

Set up conversion tracking to measure the actions users take after clicking on your ads, such as purchases, form submissions, or phone calls. This data enables you to calculate your ROI and optimize your campaigns accordingly.

4.4.6 Optimize Your Landing Pages

Ensure your landing pages are relevant to your ad copy and keywords, providing a seamless user experience and increasing the likelihood of conversion. Consider using Google Analytics or Google Optimize to test and improve your landing page performance.

4.4.7 Explore Advanced Targeting and Bidding Strategies

Leverage Google Ads' advanced targeting and bidding options, such as remarketing, in-market audiences, or target CPA bidding, to refine your campaigns and maximize your ROI.

In conclusion, Google Ads is a powerful advertising platform that offers businesses increased online visibility, targeted advertising, and measurable results. By following the steps outlined in this chapter and implementing best practices, you can create effective ad campaigns that drive traffic, generate leads, and ultimately grow your business.

TL ; DR

Google Ads is a powerful online advertising platform that allows businesses to create targeted ads on Google Search, Google

Display Network, and YouTube using a pay-per-click model. Google Ads offers increased online visibility, precise targeting, measurable results, budget control, and flexibility. To get started, create a Google Ads account, set up your campaign, create ad groups, write compelling ad copy, add ad extensions, and launch your campaign. Maximize success by conducting thorough keyword research, focusing on ad quality, using negative keywords, testing ad copy, implementing conversion tracking, optimizing landing pages, and exploring advanced targeting and bidding strategies.

Google Analytics

5.1 What is Google Analytics?

Google Analytics is a robust web analytics platform that allows businesses to collect, analyze, and visualize data about their website's traffic, user behavior, and overall performance. It provides valuable insights into your audience, including demographics, interests, and geographical location. With Google Analytics, business owners can identify trends, track conversions, measure the effectiveness of marketing campaigns, and make data-driven decisions to optimize their online presence.

5.2 The Importance of Google Analytics for Business Owners

Google Analytics offers numerous benefits to business owners, including:

5.2.1 Informed Decision Making

By analyzing your website's data, you can make informed decisions about your marketing strategies, website design, content creation, and overall business direction.

5.2.2 Enhanced User Experience

Understanding how users interact with your website enables you to identify areas for improvement, optimize your site's layout and navigation, and provide a better user experience.

5.2.3 Measuring Marketing Campaigns

Google Analytics allows you to track the performance of your online marketing campaigns, identify which channels drive the most traffic and conversions, and allocate your resources more effectively.

5.2.4 Improved Conversion Rates

Identify the factors that influence your website's conversion rates, such as landing page design, user behavior, or traffic sources, and implement data-driven changes to increase your conversions.

5.2.5 Real-Time Data

Google Analytics provides real-time data, giving you instant access to your website's performance and enabling you to respond quickly to any issues or opportunities.

5.3 How to Get Started with Google Analytics

To set up Google Analytics for your website, follow these steps:

5.3.1 Create a Google Analytics Account

Visit the Google Analytics website (https://analytics.google.com/) and sign in with your Google account. If you don't have an account, create one by following the prompts.

5.3.2 Set Up a Property

After signing in, click "Start measuring" and create a new property by entering your website's name, URL, industry category, and time zone. Click "Create" to complete the setup process.

5.3.3 Install the Tracking Code

Google Analytics will generate a unique tracking code for your website. Copy this code and paste it into the HTML of every page on your site, preferably within the <head> section.

5.3.4 Configure Your Account Settings

Customize your Google Analytics account settings, such as data retention periods, user access levels, and linking with other Google products like Google Ads or Google Search Console.

5.3.5 Set Up Goals

Goals in Google Analytics allow you to track specific user actions, such as form submissions or online purchases. Set up goals to measure your website's conversion rates and monitor the success of your marketing efforts.

5.4 Navigating Google Analytics Reports

Google Analytics offers a wide range of reports, organized into the following categories:

5.4.1 Real-Time Reports

Real-time reports display your website's current activity, such as the number of active users, the pages they are viewing, and their locations.

5.4.2 Audience Reports

Audience reports provide insights into your website's visitors, including demographics, interests, behavior, and technology used.

5.4.3 Acquisition Reports

Acquisition reports show how users find your website, detailing traffic sources, channels, and the performance of your online marketing campaigns.

5.4.4 Behavior Reports

Behavior reports analyze how users interact with your website, such as the pages they visit, the time they spend on each page, and the content they engage with.

5.4.5 Conversions Reports

Conversions reports track your website's
Conversions reports track your website's goal
completions, e-commerce transactions, and
other significant user actions that contribute to
your business objectives.

5.5 Tips for Maximizing Google Analytics Insights

To make the most of Google Analytics,
consider the following best practices:

5.5.1 Segment Your Data

Apply segments to your reports to analyze
specific subsets of your data, such as traffic
from a particular source or users who have
completed a specific action.

5.5.2 Set Up Custom Alerts

Create custom alerts to receive notifications
when significant changes occur in your data,
such as a sudden increase in traffic or a drop in
conversions.

5.5.3 Use Annotations

Add annotations to your reports to document important events, such as website updates, marketing campaigns, or industry news, providing context to your data and helping to identify trends or anomalies.

5.5.4 Connect Google Analytics with Other Google Products

Link your Google Analytics account with other Google products, such as Google Ads or Google Search Console, to access additional data and insights.

5.5.5 Regularly Review Your Reports

Schedule regular reviews of your Google Analytics reports to stay informed about your website's performance, identify opportunities for improvement, and make data-driven decisions.

In conclusion, Google Analytics is an essential tool for business owners to understand their website's performance, user behavior, and the effectiveness of their marketing efforts. By setting up Google Analytics, configuring your account settings, and exploring the platform's diverse reporting capabilities, you can make informed decisions that drive business growth and improve your online presence.

TL;DR

Google Analytics is a powerful web analytics platform that enables businesses to collect, analyze, and visualize data about their website's traffic, user behavior, and performance. It is important for informed decision making, enhancing user experience, measuring marketing campaigns, improving conversion rates, and accessing real-time data. To get started, create a Google Analytics account, set up a property, install the tracking code, configure your account settings, and set up goals. Maximize insights by segmenting data, setting up custom alerts, using annotations, connecting with other Google products, and regularly reviewing reports.

Google Search Console

6.1 What is Google Search Console?

Google Search Console (formerly known as Google Webmaster Tools) is a free web service provided by Google that helps website owners monitor, maintain, and troubleshoot their site's presence in Google Search results. It provides valuable insights into your website's search performance, indexing status, organic search traffic, and technical issues. With Google Search Console, business owners can optimize their website for search engines, improve their search visibility, and enhance the user experience.

6.2 The Importance of Google Search Console for Business Owners

Google Search Console offers numerous benefits to business owners, including:

6.2.1 Improved Search Engine Optimization (SEO)

Google Search Console provides insights into your website's organic search performance, such as your top-performing keywords, click-through rates, and average search rankings. This information can help you optimize your site's content and SEO strategy.

6.2.2 Indexing and Crawling Management

Monitor and control how Google crawls and indexes your website, submit sitemaps, and request indexing for new or updated content.

6.2.3 Identification of Technical Issues

Google Search Console alerts you to any technical issues that may affect your website's search performance, such as broken links, mobile usability problems, or security issues.

6.2.4 Enhanced User Experience

By identifying and resolving technical issues, improving your site's search performance, and optimizing your content, you can provide a better user experience for your website visitors.

6.3 How to Get Started with Google Search Console

To set up Google Search Console for your website, follow these steps:

6.3.1 Create a Google Search Console Account

Visit the Google Search Console website (https://search.google.com/search-console/) and sign in with your Google account. If you don't have an account, create one by following the prompts.

6.3.2 Add Your Website

After signing in, click "Add property" and enter your website's URL. Google Search Console supports two types of properties: URL prefix (specific to a single URL format) and Domain (covers all subdomains and protocols). Choose the most suitable option for your website.

6.3.3 Verify Ownership

To confirm that you own the website, Google Search Console offers several verification methods, such as uploading an HTML file, adding a meta tag, or updating your DNS records. Choose the most convenient method and follow the instructions provided.

6.3.4 Submit Your Sitemap

A sitemap is an XML file that lists your website's URLs, helping Google discover and crawl your content. If you have a sitemap, submit it to Google Search Console to improve your site's indexing.

6.4 Navigating Google Search Console Reports

Google Search Console offers a range of reports and tools, organized into the following categories:

6.4.1 Performance Report

The Performance report displays your website's search performance data, such as the total number of clicks, impressions, average click-through rate (CTR), and average position for your organic search results.

6.4.2 URL Inspection Tool

The URL Inspection tool allows you to check the indexing status and crawlability of a specific URL on your website, as well as request indexing for new or updated content.

6.4.3 Coverage Report

The Coverage report shows the indexing status of your website's URLs, including any errors, warnings, or excluded pages.

6.4.4 Sitemaps Report

The Sitemaps report allows you to submit, remove, and monitor the status of your website's sitemaps.

6.4.5 Mobile Usability Report

The Mobile Usability report identifies any issues with your website's mobile-friendliness, such as viewport configuration problems or content sizing issues.

6.4.6 Core Web Vitals Report

The Core Web Vitals report provides insights into your website's user experience metrics, such as loading speed, interactivity, and visual stability.

6.4.7 Security & Manual Actions

The Security & Manual Actions section alerts you to any security issues affecting your website or manual actions taken by Google due to policy violations.

6.4.8 Links Report

The Links report displays information about the external and internal links pointing to your website, helping you understand your site's backlink profile and internal linking structure.

6.5 Tips for Maximizing Google Search Console Insights

To make the most of Google Search Console, consider the following best practices:

6.5.1 Monitor Your Performance Regularly

Regularly review your Performance report to stay informed about your website's search performance and identify opportunities for improvement.

6.5.2 Fix Technical Issues Promptly

Address any technical issues reported in Google Search Console as soon as possible to maintain your website's search visibility and user experience.

6.5.3 Optimize Your Content

Use the insights from your Performance report to optimize your website's content, focusing on high-performing keywords, improving CTR, and increasing your search rankings.

6.5.4 Monitor Mobile Usability

With the growing importance of mobile search, ensure that your website is mobile-friendly by regularly reviewing the Mobile Usability report and addressing any issues.

6.5.5 Improve User Experience

Use the Core Web Vitals report to identify and resolve user experience issues, such as slow loading times or poor interactivity, which can affect your search rankings.

In conclusion, Google Search Console is a vital tool for business owners to monitor and optimize their website's search performance, identify and resolve technical issues, and enhance the user experience. By setting up Google Search Console, verifying your website ownership, and exploring the platform's diverse reporting capabilities, you can make informed decisions that drive business growth and improve your online presence.

TL ; DR

Google Search Console is a free web service that helps website owners monitor, maintain, and troubleshoot their site's presence in Google Search results. It is crucial for improving SEO, managing indexing and crawling, identifying technical issues, and enhancing user experience. To get started, create a Google Search Console account, add your website, verify ownership, and submit your sitemap. Maximize insights by regularly monitoring performance, fixing technical issues promptly, optimizing content, monitoring mobile usability, and improving user experience.

Google Trends

7.1 What is Google Trends?

Google Trends is a free online tool provided by Google that allows users to explore and analyze the popularity of search queries across different regions, languages, and time periods. By visualizing search data, Google Trends helps users identify trends, patterns, and seasonal fluctuations in search behavior. For business owners, Google Trends can be a valuable resource for market research, content creation, and marketing strategy development.

7.2 The Importance of Google Trends for Business Owners

Google Trends offers numerous benefits to business owners, including:

7.2.1 Market Research

Google Trends allows you to analyze search data for your industry, helping you understand market dynamics, identify emerging trends, and anticipate customer needs.

7.2.2 Content Creation

By discovering popular topics and trending search queries, you can create relevant, timely, and engaging content that resonates with your target audience.

7.2.3 Marketing Strategy Development

Google Trends can help you identify the best times to launch marketing campaigns, adjust your advertising budget, or introduce new products based on seasonal search patterns.

7.2.4 Competitor Analysis

Analyze search trends for your competitors' brand names or products to gain insights into their online presence, market share, and customer interest.

7.2.5 Keyword Research

Google Trends can supplement your keyword research efforts by providing insights into the search volume, popularity, and seasonality of specific search queries.

7.3 How to Get Started with Google Trends

To start using Google Trends, follow these steps:

7.3.1 Visit the Google Trends Website

Access Google Trends by visiting https://trends.google.com/. You do not need a Google account to use the tool.

7.3.2 Enter a Search Query

Enter a search term, topic, or keyword into the search bar at the top of the page. Google Trends will display a graph showing the search interest over time for the entered query.

7.3.3 Refine Your Search

Use the filters provided to customize your search by time range, location, category, and search type (e.g., web search, image search, news search, or YouTube search).

7.3.4 Compare Multiple Queries

Add up to four additional search queries to compare their search interest over time, helping you identify the most popular or fastest-growing trends.

7.3.5 Explore Related Queries

Google Trends displays a list of related queries, which can provide additional insights into user search behavior and help you discover new keywords or topics.

7.4 Tips for Maximizing Google Trends Insights

To make the most of Google Trends, consider the following best practices:

7.4.1 Regularly Monitor Trends

Stay informed about the latest trends and search patterns in your industry by regularly reviewing Google Trends data.

7.4.2 Use Google Trends in Combination with Other Tools

Combine Google Trends with other keyword research and SEO tools, such as Google Ads Keyword Planner or Google Analytics, to gain a comprehensive understanding of your target audience's search behavior.

7.4.3 Pay Attention to Seasonality

Identify seasonal fluctuations in search interest for your products or services, and use this information to optimize your marketing strategy and budget allocation.

7.4.4 Leverage Trending Topics for Content Creation

Create timely and relevant content based on trending topics or search queries to capture your audience's attention and boost your online visibility.

In conclusion, Google Trends is a powerful tool for business owners to understand search behavior, identify trends, and make informed decisions about content creation and marketing strategy. By getting started with Google Trends and leveraging its insights, you can stay ahead of the curve, capitalize on emerging trends, and grow your business.

TL ; DR

Google Trends is a free online tool that helps users analyze the popularity of search queries across different regions, languages, and time periods. It is essential for business owners for market research, content creation, marketing strategy development, competitor analysis, and keyword research. To get started, visit the Google Trends website, enter a search query, refine your search using filters, and compare multiple queries. Maximize insights by regularly monitoring trends, using Google Trends in combination with other tools, paying attention to seasonality, and leveraging trending topics for content creation.

Google Tag Manager

8.1 What is Google Tag Manager?

Google Tag Manager (GTM) is a free tag management system provided by Google that allows you to easily manage and deploy various tracking and marketing tags on your website without having to modify the site's code directly. Tags are snippets of code that are used to collect data or integrate third-party tools, such as Google Analytics, Google Ads, or other marketing and analytics services. By using Google Tag Manager, business owners can streamline their tag implementation process, improve website performance, and gain more control over their tracking and marketing efforts.

8.2 The Importance of Google Tag Manager for Business Owners

Google Tag Manager offers numerous benefits to business owners, including:

8.2.1 Simplified Tag Management

Easily add, update, or remove tags on your website without needing to edit the site's code or rely on web developers, saving time and reducing the risk of errors.

8.2.2 Improved Website Performance

By consolidating your tags into a single container, Google Tag Manager can help improve your website's loading speed and overall performance.

8.2.3 Enhanced Data Accuracy

Google Tag Manager ensures that your tags are consistently deployed across your site, resulting in more accurate data collection and reporting.

8.2.4 Increased Flexibility

With a wide range of pre-built tag templates and the ability to create custom tags, Google Tag Manager offers greater flexibility and control over your tracking and marketing efforts.

8.2.5 Version Control and Collaboration

Google Tag Manager provides version control, enabling you to track changes, roll back to previous versions, and collaborate with team members.

8.3 How to Get Started with Google Tag Manager

To start using Google Tag Manager, follow these steps:

8.3.1 Create a Google Tag Manager Account

Visit the Google Tag Manager website (https://tagmanager.google.com/) and sign in with your Google account. If you don't have an account, create one by following the prompts.

8.3.2 Create a New Container

After signing in, create a new container for your website by clicking "Create Account," entering your account and container names, and selecting the "Web" target platform.

8.3.3 Install the Container Code

Google Tag Manager will provide you with a container snippet, which consists of two code sections. Add these code sections to your website's source code: the first part should be placed as close to the opening <head> tag as possible, and the second part should be placed immediately after the opening <body> tag.

8.3.4 Add Tags to Your Container

In the Google Tag Manager interface, click "Add a new tag," choose a tag template or create a custom tag, and configure the tag settings. Set up triggers to determine when the tag should fire, such as when a page loads or when a user clicks a specific button.

8.3.5 Publish Your Changes

After adding your tags and configuring your triggers, click "Submit" to publish your changes and make your tags live on your website.

8.4 Tips for Maximizing Google Tag Manager Benefits

To make the most of Google Tag Manager, consider the following best practices:

8.4.1 Organize Your Tags and Triggers

Use a consistent naming convention for your tags and triggers, and group related items in folders to keep your Google Tag Manager workspace organized and easy to navigate.

8.4.2 Test Your Tags Before Publishing

Use Google Tag Manager's "Preview" mode to test your tags and ensure they are firing correctly before publishing your changes.

8.4.3 Monitor and Optimize Your Tags

Regularly review your tags' performance and make any necessary updates or optimizations to improve your website's performance and data accuracy.

8.4.4 Use Variables for Efficiency

Utilize built-in and custom variables in Google Tag Manager to streamline your tag configuration process and minimize the need for repetitive manual input.

8.4.5 Leverage the Community Template Gallery

Explore the Community Template Gallery to find pre-built templates for various third-party tags, which can save you time and simplify the tag implementation process.

8.4.6 Implement Tag Firing Priorities

Assign firing priorities to your tags to control the order in which they are executed, ensuring that critical tags fire before less important ones.

8.4.7 Ensure Compliance with Privacy Regulations

Make sure your tag implementations comply with applicable privacy regulations, such as the General Data Protection Regulation (GDPR) or the California Consumer Privacy Act (CCPA), by implementing consent management solutions and configuring your tags accordingly.

In conclusion, Google Tag Manager is a powerful tool that simplifies the tag management process, improves website performance, and gives business owners greater control over their tracking and marketing efforts. By getting started with Google Tag Manager and following best practices, you can streamline your analytics and marketing processes, ensuring accurate data collection and better decision-making for your business.

TL ; DR

Google Tag Manager (GTM) is a free tag management system that allows business owners to easily manage and deploy tracking and marketing tags on their websites without editing the site's code directly. GTM is essential for simplified tag management, improved website performance, enhanced data accuracy, increased flexibility, and version control. To get started, create a GTM account, create a container, install the container code on your website, add tags and configure triggers, and publish your changes. Maximize benefits by organizing your tags and triggers, testing tags before publishing, monitoring and optimizing tags, using variables, leveraging the Community Template Gallery, implementing tag firing priorities, and ensuring compliance with privacy regulations.

Google Merchant Center

9.1 What is Google Merchant Center?

Google Merchant Center is a free online platform that enables retailers to upload and manage their product data for use across various Google services, such as Google Shopping, Google Ads, and Google Search. By integrating your e-commerce store with Google Merchant Center, you can showcase your products across multiple Google channels, reach a wider audience, and drive more sales.

9.2 The Importance of Google Merchant Center for Business Owners

Google Merchant Center offers numerous benefits to business owners, including:

9.2.1 Increased Visibility

By uploading your products to Google Merchant Center, your items can appear in

Google Search results, Google Shopping, and Google Ads, increasing your brand's visibility and attracting more potential customers.

9.2.2 Enhanced Shopping Experience

Google Merchant Center allows you to provide detailed product information, such as images, descriptions, and pricing, which can improve the shopping experience for users and lead to higher conversion rates.

9.2.3 Streamlined Product Management

Easily manage and update your product data in one central location, ensuring that your product information remains accurate and up-to-date across all Google platforms.

9.2.4 Customized Product Feeds

Create customized product feeds for specific campaigns or target audiences, allowing you to better tailor your marketing efforts and reach your desired customers.

9.2.5 Integration with Google Ads

Leverage your product data in Google Merchant Center to create dynamic Google Ads campaigns, such as Shopping Ads and Smart Shopping campaigns, which can help drive more sales and improve your return on investment.

9.3 How to Get Started with Google Merchant Center

To start using Google Merchant Center, follow these steps:

9.3.1 Create a Google Merchant Center Account

Visit the Google Merchant Center website (https://merchants.google.com/) and sign in with your Google account. If you don't have an account, create one by following the prompts.

9.3.2 Set Up Your Merchant Center Account

Once logged in, complete the initial setup process by providing your business information, such as your business name, website URL, and contact details. Also, configure your tax and shipping settings according to your business's requirements.

9.3.3 Verify and Claim Your Website

Verify your website ownership in Google Merchant Center by using one of the available methods, such as adding a meta tag to your site's homepage or uploading an HTML file. Once verified, claim your website to confirm your association with the site.

9.3.4 Create and Upload Your Product Feed

Prepare a product feed containing detailed information about your products, including product IDs, titles, descriptions, images, prices, and availability. Format your product feed as a text (.txt) or XML (.xml) file, and upload it to Google Merchant Center using one of the supported methods, such as manual upload, scheduled fetch, or Google Sheets.

9.3.5 Set Up Google Ads Integration (Optional)

If you plan to use your product data for Google Ads campaigns, link your Google Ads account to your Merchant Center account by following the on-screen instructions.

9.4 Tips for Maximizing Google Merchant Center Benefits

To make the most of Google Merchant Center, consider the following best practices:

9.4.1 Optimize Your Product Data

Ensure your product titles, descriptions, and images are accurate, informative, and appealing to potential customers. Include relevant keywords to improve your products' visibility in search results.

9.4.2 Monitor and Resolve Disapprovals

Regularly check your Google Merchant Center account for any disapproved products, and address the issues promptly to maintain your product listings' visibility and compliance with Google's policies.

9.4.3 Use Product Ratings and Reviews

Enable product ratings and reviews in your Google Merchant Center account to enhance your products' credibility and increase the likelihood of conversions.

9.4.4 Leverage Promotions and Special Offers

Utilize promotions and special offers, such as discounts or free shipping, to entice potential customers and encourage them to purchase your products.

9.4.5 Keep Your Product Feed Up-to-Date

Regularly update your product feed to ensure accurate pricing, availability, and product information, which can help prevent potential customer dissatisfaction and improve your store's reputation.

9.4.6 Monitor Your Performance

Use Google Merchant Center's performance reports to track the effectiveness of your product listings and identify areas for improvement or optimization.

In conclusion, Google Merchant Center is a valuable tool that can help business owners increase their products' visibility, improve the shopping experience for users, and ultimately drive more sales. By getting started with Google Merchant Center and following best practices, you can effectively manage your product data, reach a wider audience, and optimize your e-commerce performance.

TL ; DR

Google Merchant Center is a free online platform that allows retailers to upload and manage their product data across various Google services, including Google Shopping, Google Ads, and Google Search. It is essential for business owners to increase product visibility, enhance the shopping experience, streamline product management, create customized product feeds, and integrate with Google Ads. To get started, create a Google Merchant Center account, set up your account, verify and claim your website, create and upload your product feed, and optionally set up Google Ads integration. Maximize benefits by optimizing your product data, monitoring and resolving disapprovals, using product ratings and reviews, leveraging promotions, keeping your product feed up-to-date, and monitoring your performance.

Google Optimize

10.1 What is Google Optimize?

Google Optimize is a free website optimization tool that enables business owners to conduct A/B testing, multivariate testing, and personalization on their websites. With Google Optimize, you can create and test different variations of your web pages, analyze their performance, and determine the most effective layouts, designs, or content for your target audience. By continually refining your website through testing, you can improve user experience, increase engagement, and ultimately drive more conversions and sales.

10.2 The Importance of Google Optimize for Business Owners

Google Optimize offers numerous benefits to business owners, including:

10.2.1 Data-Driven Decision Making

By conducting tests and analyzing the results, you can make informed decisions about your website's design, content, and functionality, ensuring that you're providing the best possible experience for your users.

10.2.2 Improved User Experience

Optimizing your website through testing can lead to a better user experience, which can result in higher engagement, longer session durations, and lower bounce rates.

10.2.3 Increased Conversions and Sales

Through testing and optimization, you can identify the most effective elements of your website, which can help you drive more conversions, sales, and revenue for your business.

10.2.4 Reduced Risk of Negative Changes

By testing proposed changes before implementing them, you can minimize the risk of making adjustments that may negatively impact your website's performance.

10.2.5 Seamless Integration with Google Analytics

Google Optimize integrates with Google Analytics, allowing you to leverage your existing data and gain deeper insights into the performance of your website and its variations.

10.3 How to Get Started with Google Optimize

To start using Google Optimize, follow these steps:

10.3.1 Create a Google Optimize Account

Visit the Google Optimize website (https://optimize.google.com/) and sign in with your Google account. If you don't have an account, create one by following the prompts.

10.3.2 Link Google Optimize to Google Analytics

After signing in, link your Google Optimize account to your Google Analytics property. This integration allows you to access your existing data and use it in your experiments.

10.3.3 Install the Google Optimize Extension

Download and install the Google Optimize extension for Google Chrome, which enables you to create and edit your experiments directly on your website.

10.3.4 Create an Experiment

In the Google Optimize interface, click "Create experiment," and select the type of experiment you want to run (A/B test, multivariate test, or personalization). Enter the details for your experiment, such as its name, objective, and the web page URL you want to test.

10.3.5 Design Your Variations

Using the Google Optimize extension, create and edit variations of your web page by adjusting elements like text, images, colors, or layout. Save your changes and return to the Google Optimize interface.

10.3.6 Configure Your Experiment Settings

Set up your experiment's targeting rules, such as defining specific audiences or determining the percentage of users who will be exposed to the test. Configure any additional settings as needed.

10.3.7 Launch Your Experiment

Once your experiment is set up, click "Start" to begin running the test. Monitor your experiment's performance in the Google Optimize interface, and analyze the results to determine which variation is the most effective.

10.3.8 Implement Winning Variations

After your experiment has concluded and you've identified the best-performing variation, implement the changes on your website to benefit from the improved user experience and increased conversions.

10.4 To make the most of Google Optimize, consider the following best practices:

10.4.1 Define Clear Objectives

Before starting an experiment, clearly define the objectives you want to achieve, such as increasing conversions, reducing bounce rates, or improving user engagement. This will help you focus your testing efforts and measure the success of your experiments.

10.4.2 Test One Variable at a Time

For A/B tests, try to test only one variable at a time, such as changing a headline, button color, or image. This will help you isolate the impact of each change and identify the specific factors that influence your website's performance.

10.4.3 Use a Representative Sample Size

Ensure that your experiments have a sufficient sample size to generate statistically significant results. This can help you make more accurate and reliable decisions based on your test data.

10.4.4 Run Experiments for an Appropriate Duration

Allow your experiments to run for an appropriate duration to collect enough data and minimize the influence of external factors, such as seasonality or short-term trends.

10.4.5 Analyze and Learn from Your Results

After each experiment, thoroughly analyze the results and draw insights from the data. Use these insights to inform your future experiments and continually refine your website's performance.

10.4.6 Iterate and Optimize

Optimization is an ongoing process. Continue to run experiments and make improvements based on your findings, striving to enhance your website's user experience and increase conversions over time.

In conclusion, Google Optimize is a powerful tool that enables business owners to conduct A/B testing, multivariate testing, and personalization on their websites to improve user experience and drive more conversions. By getting started with Google Optimize and following best practices, you can make data-driven decisions, minimize the risk of negative changes, and continually refine your website's performance to better serve your customers and grow your business.

TL ; DR

Google Optimize is a free website optimization tool that allows business owners to conduct A/B testing, multivariate testing, and personalization on their websites. It is essential for making data-driven decisions, improving user experience, increasing conversions, reducing the risk of negative changes, and integrating with Google Analytics. To get started, create a Google Optimize account, link it to Google Analytics, install the Google Optimize extension, create and design experiments, configure experiment settings, and launch the experiment. Maximize benefits by defining clear objectives, testing one variable at a time, using representative sample sizes, running experiments for an appropriate duration, analyzing results, and iterating to optimize your website continuously.

Google Data Studio

11.1 What is Google Data Studio?

Google Data Studio is a free, cloud-based data visualization and reporting tool that enables business owners to create interactive and customizable dashboards and reports. By connecting various data sources, such as Google Analytics, Google Sheets, or Google Ads, you can transform raw data into visually appealing and easily digestible insights. Google Data Studio simplifies data analysis, enables collaboration, and allows you to make data-driven decisions more effectively.

11.2 The Importance of Google Data Studio for Business Owners

Google Data Studio offers numerous benefits for business owners, including:

11.2.1 Simplified Data Analysis

By presenting data in a visual format, Google Data Studio makes it easier to understand complex datasets and identify trends, patterns, or outliers.

11.2.2 Customization and Flexibility

Google Data Studio offers a range of customization options, allowing you to tailor your dashboards and reports to meet your specific needs and preferences.

11.2.3 Seamless Data Integration

Google Data Studio connects to various data sources, making it easy to consolidate and analyze data from multiple platforms in one place.

11.2.4 Real-Time Data Updates

As a cloud-based tool, Google Data Studio automatically updates your dashboards and reports with the latest data, ensuring that you always have access to the most recent information.

11.2.5 Collaboration and Sharing

Google Data Studio enables you to collaborate with team members and share your dashboards and reports with stakeholders, improving communication and transparency within your organization.

11.3 How to Get Started with Google Data Studio

To start using Google Data Studio, follow these steps:

11.3.1 Create a Google Data Studio Account

Visit the Google Data Studio website (https://datastudio.google.com/) and sign in with your Google account. If you don't have an account, create one by following the prompts.

11.3.2 Explore the Interface

Familiarize yourself with the Google Data Studio interface, which includes the home page, where you can access your reports and data sources, and the report editor, where you can create and customize your dashboards.

11.3.3 Connect a Data Source

To connect a data source, click "Create" on the home page, then select "Data Source." Choose from the available connectors, such as Google Analytics, Google Sheets, or Google Ads, and authorize access to your data.

11.3.4 Create a New Report

Click "Create" on the home page, then select "Report." Choose a data source for your report and click "Add to Report." This will open the report editor.

11.3.5 Design Your Dashboard

In the report editor, use the available tools to add charts, tables, graphs, or other visualizations to your dashboard. Customize the appearance and formatting of your visualizations, and apply filters or date ranges as needed.

11.3.6 Share Your Report

To share your report with others, click "Share" in the top right corner of the report editor. Enter the email addresses of your intended recipients, and adjust the sharing settings as desired.

11.4 Tips for Maximizing Google Data Studio Benefits

To make the most of Google Data Studio, consider the following best practices:

11.4.1 Start with a Clear Objective

Before creating a dashboard or report, identify the key metrics and insights you want to track and communicate. This will help you design a focused and effective dashboard.

11.4.2 Use Appropriate Visualizations

Choose the right visualization type for your data, such as bar charts for comparing categories, line charts for displaying trends over time, or pie charts for illustrating proportions.

11.4.3 Keep It Simple

Avoid cluttering your dashboard with too many visualizations or excessive information. Keep your design clean and simple to ensure that your data is easy to understand and interpret.

11.4.4 Make Use of Templates

Google Data Studio offers a variety of pre-built templates that you can use as a starting point for your own dashboards. Explore these templates and customize them to suit your specific needs.

11.4.5 Leverage Custom Calculations and Formulas

Google Data Studio allows you to create custom calculations and formulas to derive new insights from your data. Make use of these features to uncover hidden trends or relationships that may not be immediately apparent.

11.4.6 Continually Refine Your Dashboards

As your business evolves and your data needs change, review and update your dashboards to ensure they remain relevant and useful.

11.4.7 Train Your Team

Ensure that your team members are familiar with Google Data Studio and its features. This will enable them to effectively use the tool to analyze data and make informed decisions.

In conclusion, Google Data Studio is a powerful data visualization and reporting tool that enables business owners to create interactive dashboards and reports, simplifying data analysis and promoting data-driven decision-making. By getting started with Google Data Studio and following best practices, you can leverage the tool's capabilities to consolidate data, communicate insights, and foster collaboration within your organization.

TL ; DR

Google Data Studio is a free, cloud-based data visualization and reporting tool that helps business owners create interactive dashboards and reports by connecting various data sources like Google Analytics, Google Sheets, and Google Ads. It simplifies data analysis, offers customization and flexibility, seamlessly integrates data, provides real-time updates, and enables collaboration and sharing. To get started, create a Google Data Studio account, explore the interface, connect a data source, create a new report, design your dashboard, and share your report. Maximize the tool's benefits by setting clear objectives, using appropriate visualizations, keeping your design simple, leveraging templates, using custom calculations, refining your dashboards regularly, and training your team.

Google Alerts

12.1 What are Google Alerts?

Google Alerts is a free, web-based service that allows you to monitor the web for new content related to specific keywords or phrases. Once you set up an alert, you will receive email notifications whenever Google discovers new content that matches your search criteria. Google Alerts helps you stay informed about industry news, brand mentions, competitor activities, or any other topic that interests you.

12.2 The Importance of Google Alerts for Business Owners

Google Alerts offers numerous benefits for business owners, including:

12.2.1 Brand Monitoring

Track mentions of your brand across the web to gauge public perception, discover customer feedback, and identify opportunities for engagement.

12.2.2 Competitor Analysis

Monitor your competitors' activities to stay informed about their latest products, promotions, or news and identify potential areas for improvement or differentiation.

12.2.3 Industry News and Trends

Stay up-to-date with the latest news, trends, and developments in your industry to make informed decisions and identify opportunities for growth.

12.2.4 Content Curation and Inspiration

Discover interesting and relevant content that you can share on your social media channels or use as inspiration for your own content creation efforts.

12.2.5 Reputation Management

Identify and address negative reviews, articles, or comments about your brand to maintain a positive reputation and address potential issues promptly.

12.3 How to Get Started with Google Alerts

Setting up Google Alerts is quick and easy. Follow these steps:

12.3.1 Visit Google Alerts

Go to the Google Alerts website (https://www.google.com/alerts) and sign in with your Google account.

12.3.2 Enter Your Search Query

In the "Create an alert about" field, enter the keywords or phrases you want to monitor, such as your brand name, product, or industry terms.

12.3.3 Customize Alert Options

Click "Show options" to configure your alert preferences, such as the frequency of notifications, sources to monitor, language, region, and email address for delivery.

12.3.4 Create Your Alert

Click "Create Alert" to save your settings and start receiving notifications for new content related to your search query.

12.3.5 Manage Your Alerts

You can view, edit, or delete your existing alerts by visiting the Google Alerts website and clicking on the respective options next to each alert.

12.4 Tips for Maximizing Google Alerts Benefits

To make the most of Google Alerts, consider the following best practices:

12.4.1 Be Specific with Your Keywords

Choose specific keywords or phrases that accurately represent the content you want to monitor. This will help you receive more relevant and targeted notifications.

12.4.2 Use Advanced Search Operators

Refine your search queries by using advanced search operators, such as quotation marks for exact phrases, a minus sign to exclude specific words, or the "site:" operator to limit your search to a particular domain.

12.4.3 Experiment with Different Alert Settings

Adjust your alert settings, such as frequency or sources, to find the optimal balance between relevance and volume of notifications.

12.4.4 Monitor Multiple Keywords

Create separate alerts for different keywords or phrases to ensure comprehensive coverage of your brand, competitors, and industry.

12.4.5 Act on Relevant Alerts

Use the information from your alerts to take action, such as engaging with customers, addressing negative feedback, or adjusting your marketing strategy based on industry trends.

In conclusion, Google Alerts is a valuable tool that enables business owners to monitor the web for new content related to their brand, competitors, or industry. By setting up and customizing alerts, you can stay informed, manage your reputation, and make data-driven decisions to grow your business. By implementing best practices, such as using specific keywords, employing advanced search operators, experimenting with alert settings, monitoring multiple keywords, and acting on relevant alerts, you can maximize the benefits of Google Alerts and maintain a competitive edge in your industry.

TL ; DR

Google Alerts is a free service that helps business owners monitor the web for new content related to specific keywords or phrases, providing valuable insights into brand mentions, competitor activities, industry news, and content curation. To get started, visit the Google Alerts website, enter your search query, customize alert options, and create your alert. Maximize the benefits of Google Alerts by using specific keywords, advanced search operators, experimenting with different settings, monitoring multiple keywords, and taking action based on the information you receive.

Google Forms

13.1 What are Google Forms?

Google Forms is a free, web-based tool that allows you to create customizable online forms and surveys for various purposes, such as gathering customer feedback, conducting market research, or managing event registrations. With an easy-to-use interface and integration with Google Sheets, Google Forms simplifies data collection, organization, and analysis, enabling you to make informed decisions and improve your business operations.

13.2 The Importance of Google Forms for Business Owners

Google Forms offers numerous benefits for business owners, including:

13.2.1 Streamlined Data Collection

Create custom forms and surveys quickly and easily, without the need for technical expertise or specialized software.

13.2.2 Versatility

Google Forms can be used for a wide range of applications, from customer feedback surveys to job applications, making it a versatile tool for various business needs.

13.2.3 Real-Time Data Analysis

Responses to your forms are automatically collected in a Google Sheet, allowing you to view and analyze your data in real-time.

13.2.4 Collaboration

Collaborate with team members on form creation and data analysis, improving communication and efficiency within your organization.

13.2.5 Customization

Customize your forms with various question types, design elements, and conditional logic to create a tailored experience for your respondents.

13.3 How to Get Started with Google Forms

To start using Google Forms, follow these steps:

13.3.1 Access Google Forms

Visit the Google Forms website (https://www.google.com/forms) and sign in with your Google account. If you don't have an account, create one by following the prompts.

13.3.2 Create a New Form

Click "Blank" to create a new form from scratch, or choose from the available templates to get started quickly.

13.3.3 Customize Your Form

Add and edit questions, choose question types (e.g., multiple choice, short answer, etc.), and customize the appearance of your form using the available options.

13.3.4 Apply Conditional Logic (Optional)

Use the "Add section" feature to create sections in your form, and apply conditional logic using the "Go to section based on answer" option. This allows you to direct respondents to different sections of the form based on their answers.

13.3.5 Configure Form Settings

Click the gear icon in the top right corner to access form settings, where you can adjust response collection options, limit submissions, add a custom confirmation message, and more.

13.3.6 Share Your Form

Click the "Send" button in the top right corner to share your form via email, obtain a shareable link, or embed the form on your website.

13.3.7 Analyze Responses

Responses to your form are automatically collected in a Google Sheet, which you can access by clicking "Responses" in the form editor and selecting "View responses in Sheets."

13.4 Tips for Maximizing Google Forms Benefits

To make the most of Google Forms, consider the following best practices:

13.4.1 Keep Your Forms Concise

Limit the length and complexity of your forms to encourage participation and reduce the likelihood of incomplete or inaccurate responses.

13.4.2 Use Clear and Specific Questions

Ensure that your questions are clear, concise, and specific to collect accurate and actionable data.

13.4.3 Leverage Different Question Types

Use a variety of question types to capture different types of information and improve the user experience for your respondents.

13.4.4 Test Your Forms

Before sharing your form, test it to ensure that it functions correctly, looks professional, and provides a smooth user experience.

13.4.5 Monitor and Analyze Responses Regularly

Regularly review the responses to your forms to identify trends, gain insights, and make data-driven decisions.

13.4.6 Act on Feedback

Use the information collected from your forms to address customer concerns, improve products or services, and identify areas for growth or improvement.

13.4.7 Promote Your Forms

Share your forms on your website, social media channels, or email campaigns to increase visibility and encourage participation.

In conclusion, Google Forms is a valuable tool for business owners seeking to streamline data collection, organization, and analysis. With its versatility, real-time data analysis, and customization features, Google Forms enables you to gather valuable insights for decision-making and improving your business operations. By following the steps to get started with Google Forms and implementing best practices, you can maximize the benefits of this powerful tool and leverage the data it provides to drive your business forward.

TL ; DR

Google Forms is a free, web-based tool that allows business owners to create customizable online forms and surveys for various purposes, such as gathering customer feedback or managing event registrations. With its easy-to-use interface and integration with Google Sheets, Google Forms simplifies data collection, organization, and analysis. To get started, visit the Google Forms website, create a new form, customize it, configure settings, share the form, and analyze responses. Maximize the benefits of Google Forms by keeping forms concise, using clear and specific questions, leveraging different question types, testing your forms, monitoring responses regularly, acting on feedback, and promoting your forms.

Google Cloud Platform

14.1 What is Google Cloud Platform?

Google Cloud Platform (GCP) is a suite of cloud computing services offered by Google that provides infrastructure, platform, and software as a service (IaaS, PaaS, and SaaS) solutions. GCP enables businesses to build, deploy, and scale applications, websites, and services on the same infrastructure that powers Google's products, such as Google Search and YouTube. GCP's comprehensive range of services includes computing power, data storage, machine learning, big data analytics, and more.

14.2 The Benefits of Google Cloud Platform for Business Owners

Google Cloud Platform offers numerous benefits for businesses of all sizes, including:

14.2.1 Scalability

GCP's scalable infrastructure allows you to adjust resources on-demand, ensuring that your applications can handle fluctuations in traffic or workload without compromising performance.

14.2.2 Cost Efficiency

GCP's pay-as-you-go pricing model means that you only pay for the resources you use, helping you manage costs more effectively.

14.2.3 Security

Google's extensive security measures, such as data encryption and robust access controls, help protect your data and applications from potential threats.

14.2.4 Innovation

GCP's advanced services, such as machine learning and big data analytics, empower you to develop innovative solutions and gain a competitive edge.

14.2.5 Flexibility

GCP's support for multiple programming languages, frameworks, and tools enables you to choose the best technologies for your specific needs.

14.3 How to Get Started with Google Cloud Platform

To start using GCP, follow these steps:

14.3.1 Create a Google Cloud Platform Account

Visit the GCP website (https://cloud.google.com/) and click "Get started for free." If you don't have a Google account, you will be prompted to create one. New users typically receive a free trial credit, which can be applied to GCP services.

14.3.2 Set Up Your GCP Project

Sign in to the Google Cloud Console (https://console.cloud.google.com/), and create a new project by clicking the project dropdown and selecting "New Project." Fill in the required information and click "Create."

14.3.3 Enable GCP Services

In the Cloud Console, navigate to the "APIs & Services" dashboard and click "Enable APIs and Services" to browse available services. Enable the ones you need by clicking on them and selecting "Enable."

14.3.4 Configure Your Environment

Follow the documentation for your chosen services to set up your development environment, including installing the Google Cloud SDK, configuring authentication, and setting up client libraries.

14.3.5 Develop and Deploy Your Application

Develop your application using the GCP services you've enabled, and deploy it to the cloud by following the documentation and best practices for your specific services.

14.4 Tips for Maximizing Google Cloud Platform Benefits

To make the most of GCP, consider the following best practices:

14.4.1 Choose the Right Services

Understand your business requirements and select the appropriate GCP services to meet your specific needs.

14.4.2 Monitor Your Resources

Regularly monitor your resource usage and adjust your settings to optimize performance and cost-efficiency.

14.4.3 Leverage GCP's Advanced Features

Take advantage of GCP's advanced services, such as machine learning and big data analytics, to create innovative solutions and drive business growth.

14.4.4 Stay Updated on New Services and Features

Stay informed about new GCP services and features by following the Google Cloud blog and attending webinars or events.

14.4.5 Seek Expert Advice

If needed, consult with GCP experts or engage with the Google Cloud community to gain insights and learn best practices.

14.4.6 Invest in Training

Provide training and resources for your team members to develop the skills needed to effectively use GCP services and optimize their benefits.

14.4.7 Implement Strong Security Measures

Adhere to GCP security best practices, such as using strong authentication methods, implementing access controls, and monitoring your environment for potential threats.

14.4.8 Plan for Disaster Recovery

Design and implement a disaster recovery plan, including data backup and redundancy, to ensure business continuity in the event of unforeseen incidents.

In conclusion, Google Cloud Platform is a powerful suite of cloud computing services that offers scalability, cost-efficiency, security, innovation, and flexibility for businesses of all sizes. By following the steps to get started with GCP and implementing best practices, you can harness the power of cloud computing to build, deploy, and scale your applications and services, driving your business forward and maintaining a competitive edge.

TL ; DR

Google Cloud Platform (GCP) is a suite of cloud computing services that enables businesses to build, deploy, and scale applications and services on Google's infrastructure. GCP offers benefits such as scalability, cost efficiency, security, innovation, and flexibility. To get started, create a GCP account, set up a project, enable required services, configure your environment, and develop and deploy your application. Maximize GCP benefits by choosing the right services, monitoring resources, leveraging advanced features, staying updated, seeking expert advice, investing in training, implementing strong security measures, and planning for disaster recovery.

Google Adsense

16.1 What is Google AdSense?

Google AdSense is a free, simple way for website owners to earn money by displaying targeted ads alongside their online content. AdSense automatically selects and displays ads relevant to your content and audience, allowing you to monetize your website, blog, or online platform without the need for direct ad sales.

16.2 Why is Google AdSense Important for Business Owners?

Google AdSense offers several benefits for business owners, including:

16.2.1 Passive Income

AdSense allows you to generate passive income from your online content, helping to offset operational costs or fund growth initiatives.

16.2.2 Easy Implementation

AdSense is easy to set up and manage, requiring minimal technical expertise or ongoing maintenance.

16.2.3 Customization and Control

You have control over the types of ads displayed on your site, as well as the ad placement and appearance, ensuring they align with your brand and user experience.

16.2.4 Access to a Large Advertiser Pool

AdSense connects you with a vast network of advertisers, increasing the likelihood of ad placements and revenue generation.

16.3 How to Get Started with Google AdSense

To start using Google AdSense, follow these steps:

16.3.1 Sign Up for an AdSense Account

Visit the Google AdSense website (https://www.google.com/adsense/) and click "Get Started" to create an account. You'll need to provide your website URL, email address, and other basic information.

16.3.2 Wait for Account Approval

Google will review your application, which can take up to a few weeks. During this time, ensure your website complies with Google's AdSense Program policies (https://support.google.com/adsense/answer/4 8182).

16.3.3 Create Ad Units

Once your account is approved, sign in to your AdSense dashboard and create ad units by selecting the ad size, type, and style that best suit your website.

16.3.4 Implement Ad Code on Your Site

After creating your ad units, AdSense will generate a unique code for each one. Copy the ad code and paste it into your website's HTML where you want the ads to appear.

16.3.5 Monitor Your Performance

Use the AdSense dashboard to track your ad performance, revenue, and optimization opportunities.

16.4 Tips for Maximizing Your AdSense Earnings

To increase your AdSense revenue, consider the following best practices:

16.4.1 Create High-Quality, Engaging Content

Produce original, engaging, and regularly updated content to attract and retain visitors, increasing the likelihood of ad views and clicks.

16.4.2 Optimize Ad Placement and Design

Experiment with different ad placements, sizes, and designs to find the most effective and unobtrusive configurations for your site.

16.4.3 Balance Ad Density

Avoid cluttering your site with too many ads, which can detract from the user experience and potentially violate AdSense policies.

16.4.4 Optimize Your Site for SEO

Use search engine optimization (SEO) best practices to increase your site's visibility and attract more visitors, leading to higher ad revenue.

16.4.5 Monitor and Analyze Your Ad Performance

Regularly review your AdSense performance data and make adjustments based on your findings to optimize your ad revenue.

In conclusion, Google AdSense is a valuable tool for business owners looking to monetize their online content through targeted advertising. By following the steps to get started with AdSense and implementing best practices, you can generate passive income and maximize your ad revenue while maintaining a positive user experience for your website visitors.

TL : DR

Google AdSense is a free tool that helps website owners monetize their content by displaying targeted ads. It offers benefits like passive income, easy implementation, customization, and access to a large pool of advertisers. To get started, sign up for an AdSense account, create ad units, and implement ad code on your site. To maximize earnings, create high-quality content, optimize ad placement and design, balance ad density, optimize your site for SEO, and monitor ad performance. AdSense is a valuable tool for generating income from online content while maintaining a positive user experience.

Google Maps Platform

18.1 What is the Google Maps Platform?

The Google Maps Platform is a suite of tools and APIs (Application Programming Interfaces) that enable businesses to integrate Google Maps into their websites, applications, and services. It provides a wide range of features, such as location-based search, mapping, and routing, that can enhance the user experience and provide valuable insights into customer behavior.

18.2 Why is the Google Maps Platform Important for Business Owners?

The Google Maps Platform offers several benefits for business owners, including:

18.2.1 Enhanced User Experience

Integrating Google Maps into your website or application can provide users with an interactive and personalized experience, allowing them to easily find and interact with your business.

18.2.2 Increased Visibility

By displaying your business on Google Maps, you can increase your visibility and reach a wider audience, potentially driving more traffic and sales.

18.2.3 Valuable Insights

The Google Maps Platform provides valuable data and insights into customer behavior, such as search queries, traffic patterns, and user demographics, which can inform marketing and operational decisions.

18.2.4 Integration with Other Google Services

The Google Maps Platform seamlessly integrates with other Google services, such as Google Ads and Google Analytics, allowing you to streamline your marketing and data analysis efforts.

18.3 How to Get Started with the Google Maps Platform

To start using the Google Maps Platform, follow these steps:

18.3.1 Create a Google Cloud Account

Visit the Google Cloud website (https://cloud.google.com/) and create an account. You'll need to provide billing information, but Google offers a free tier with a limited usage quota.

18.3.2 Enable the Google Maps Platform API

In the Google Cloud Console, navigate to the API Library and enable the Google Maps Platform API you wish to use, such as Maps JavaScript API or Places API.

18.3.3 Obtain an API Key

Once you've enabled the API, you'll need to generate an API key, which will be used to authenticate your requests and track usage.

18.3.4 Integrate the Google Maps API into Your Website or Application

Use the documentation and code samples provided by Google to integrate the API into your website or application. This may involve adding JavaScript code to your website or using SDKs (Software Development Kits) for mobile app development.

18.4 Tips for Maximizing the Google Maps Platform's Potential

To get the most out of the Google Maps Platform, consider the following best practices:

18.4.1 Provide Accurate and Detailed Information

Ensure your business information is accurate and up-to-date on Google Maps, including your address, hours, and contact information.

18.4.2 Customize the Map Appearance

Use the Google Maps API to customize the appearance of your map, such as adding custom markers or changing the color scheme, to align with your brand and enhance the user experience.

18.4.3 Optimize for Mobile Devices

Ensure your maps and location-based features are optimized for mobile devices, as many users access maps on their smartphones or tablets.

18.4.4 Use Analytics to Inform Decisions

Use Google Analytics to track user behavior and engagement with your maps, allowing you to make data-driven decisions and optimize your maps for better performance.

18.4.5 Experiment with Different Features and APIs

Explore the full range of features and APIs offered by the Google Maps Platform, such as geocoding or directions, to find new ways to enhance the user experience and provide value to your customers.

In conclusion, the Google Maps Platform is a powerful tool for business owners looking to provide location-based features and insights to their customers.

TL:DR

The Google Maps Platform is a suite of tools and APIs that allow businesses to integrate Google Maps into their websites, applications, and services. It provides features such as location-based search, mapping, and routing that can enhance the user experience and provide valuable insights into customer behavior. By using the Google Maps Platform, businesses can increase their visibility, provide a personalized experience for users, and obtain valuable data to inform marketing and operational decisions. To get started, create a Google Cloud account, enable the desired API, obtain an API key, and integrate it into your website or application. Best practices include providing accurate information, customizing the map appearance, optimizing for mobile devices, using analytics to inform decisions, and experimenting with different features and APIs.

Think with Google

19.1 What is Think with Google?

Think with Google is an online resource hub designed to provide businesses with insights and trends on the latest digital marketing strategies, consumer behavior, and industry trends. It features a range of articles, case studies, research reports, and data insights that help businesses stay up-to-date and informed about the latest digital marketing trends and best practices.

19.2 Why is Think with Google Important for Business Owners?

Think with Google offers several benefits for business owners, including:

19.2.1 Access to Valuable Insights and Research

The platform provides access to valuable insights and research that can help businesses understand consumer behavior, identify industry trends, and develop effective digital marketing strategies.

19.2.2 Cost Efficiency

Think with Google is a free platform, making it an ideal solution for businesses with limited budgets.

19.2.3 Improved Digital Marketing Performance

By staying up-to-date with the latest digital marketing trends and best practices, businesses can improve their marketing performance and stay ahead of the competition.

19.2.4 Access to Case Studies and Success Stories

The platform provides access to case studies and success stories from businesses across a variety of industries, offering valuable insights and inspiration for businesses looking to improve their digital marketing efforts.

19.3 How to Get Started with Think with Google

To get started with Think with Google, follow these steps:

19.3.1 Visit the Think with Google Website

Visit the Think with Google website (https://www.thinkwithgoogle.com/) and explore the various articles, case studies, and research reports available on the platform.

19.3.2 Sign Up for Updates

Sign up for email updates to receive the latest articles, insights, and trends directly to your inbox.

19.3.3 Explore Resources by Topic

Explore the resources available on the platform by topic, such as industry trends, consumer behavior, and digital marketing strategies.

19.3.4 Apply Insights to Your Business

Apply the insights and best practices gained from the platform to your business to improve your marketing performance and stay ahead of the competition.

19.4 Tips for Maximizing the Potential of Think with Google

To get the most out of Think with Google, consider the following best practices:

19.4.1 Stay Up-to-Date

Regularly check the platform for the latest articles, case studies, and research reports to stay up-to-date with the latest digital marketing trends and best practices.

19.4.2 Apply Insights to Your Business

Apply the insights and best practices gained from the platform to your business to improve your marketing performance and stay ahead of the competition.

19.4.3 Use Case Studies and Success Stories for Inspiration

Use the case studies and success stories available on the platform for inspiration and ideas for your own digital marketing campaigns.

19.4.4 Collaborate with Your Team

Collaborate with your team to discuss the insights and best practices gained from the platform and develop effective digital marketing strategies for your business.

19.5 Conclusion

Think with Google is a valuable resource hub for business owners looking to further their Google education and stay up-to-date with the latest digital marketing trends and best practices. By following the steps to get started with Think with Google and implementing best practices, businesses can improve their marketing performance, stay ahead of the competition, and drive growth and success.

TL : DR

Think with Google is an online resource hub that provides valuable insights and research on the latest digital marketing trends, consumer behavior, and industry trends. It offers a range of articles, case studies, research reports, and data insights to help businesses improve their marketing performance, stay up-to-date, and stay ahead of the competition. The platform is free and offers tips and inspiration for businesses to apply to their own digital marketing strategies.

Google Primer

20.1 What is Google Primer?

Google Primer is a mobile application designed to provide business owners with free, bite-sized lessons on digital marketing topics. The app features interactive lessons that can be completed in just five minutes, making it an ideal solution for busy business owners who want to improve their marketing skills on-the-go.

20.2 Why is Google Primer Important for Business Owners?

Google Primer offers several benefits for business owners, including:

20.2.1 Access to Free, High-Quality Marketing Education

The app provides access to free, high-quality marketing education that can help business owners improve their marketing skills and stay up-to-date with the latest digital marketing trends and best practices.

20.2.2 Convenience and Flexibility

The app can be accessed from anywhere, allowing business owners to learn and improve their marketing skills on-the-go, at their own pace, and on their own schedule.

20.2.3 Interactive Learning

The app offers interactive learning experiences, including quizzes and case studies, to help business owners apply the lessons to their own businesses.

20.2.4 Relevant and Practical Lessons

The app offers lessons that are relevant and practical, covering topics such as SEO, social media, email marketing, and more.

20.3 How to Get Started with Google Primer

To get started with Google Primer, follow these steps:

20.3.1 Download the App

Download the Google Primer app from the App Store (for iOS) or Google Play Store (for Android).

20.3.2 Sign Up

Create an account by entering your email address and creating a password.

20.3.3 Choose a Topic

Choose a marketing topic that interests you from the list of lessons available in the app.

20.3.4 Complete a Lesson

Complete the interactive lesson by reading through the content, taking quizzes, and applying the lessons to your own business.

20.3.5 Track Your Progress

Track your progress by reviewing your completed lessons and achievements.

20.4 Tips for Maximizing the Potential of Google Primer

To get the most out of Google Primer, consider the following best practices:

20.4.1 Set Goals

Set specific goals for what you want to learn and achieve through using the app.

20.4.2 Make Time

Schedule time each day or week to complete lessons and apply the lessons to your business.

20.4.3 Apply Lessons to Your Business

Take the time to apply the lessons learned in each lesson to your own business to improve your marketing performance.

20.4.4 Complete All Lessons

Complete all lessons in a topic to gain a comprehensive understanding of the digital marketing topic.

20.5 Conclusion

Google Primer is a valuable mobile application for business owners looking to improve their marketing skills and stay up-to-date with the latest digital marketing trends and best practices. By following the steps to get started with Google Primer and implementing best practices, business owners can improve their marketing performance, drive growth and success, and stay ahead of the competition.

TL : DR

Google Primer is a mobile app designed to provide free, bite-sized lessons on digital marketing topics to help business owners improve their marketing skills on-the-go. The app offers convenient and flexible learning experiences, interactive lessons, relevant and practical lessons, and progress tracking features. The app is free and can be downloaded from the App Store or Google Play Store.

Google for Nonprofits

21.1 Introduction

Google is committed to supporting nonprofits in achieving their missions by providing them with access to a range of resources, tools, and products. The Google for Nonprofits program is designed to help organizations with nonprofit status to increase their reach, raise awareness, and drive social impact through the power of technology.

21.2 What is Google for Nonprofits?

Google for Nonprofits is a program that offers nonprofits access to a range of free and discounted Google products and services. These resources are designed to help nonprofits increase their online presence, engage with their audience, and drive donations.

21.3 What Resources are Available to Nonprofits?

The Google for Nonprofits program offers access to a range of products and services, including:

21.3.1 Google Ad Grants

Google Ad Grants is a program that offers eligible nonprofits $10,000 per month in free advertising on Google Search. This can be used to drive traffic to a nonprofit's website, promote their mission, or raise awareness about their cause.

21.3.2 Google Workspace

Google Workspace is a suite of productivity and collaboration tools that can help nonprofits to work more efficiently, communicate effectively, and stay organized. Nonprofits can access Gmail, Google Drive, Google Meet, and other tools for free.

21.3.3 YouTube Nonprofit Program

The YouTube Nonprofit Program offers nonprofits access to a range of features that can help them to tell their story, engage with their audience, and drive donations. This includes the ability to add donation cards to videos, access to live streaming, and more.

21.3.4 Google One Today

Google One Today is a mobile app that allows users to discover and donate to a different nonprofit every day. Nonprofits can register with the app to gain exposure and drive donations.

21.3.5 Google Earth Outreach

Google Earth Outreach is a program that offers nonprofits access to Google Earth and Google Maps technologies. Nonprofits can use these tools to create interactive maps and visualizations that showcase their work and impact.

21.4 How to Get Started with Google for Nonprofits

To get started with Google for Nonprofits, follow these steps:

21.4.1 Check Eligibility

Check if your nonprofit is eligible for the program by visiting the Google for Nonprofits website (https://www.google.com/nonprofits/eligibility/).

21.4.2 Apply

Submit an application for the program by filling out the online form and providing proof of your nonprofit status.

21.4.3 Wait for Approval

Wait for Google to review and approve your application, which can take up to two weeks.

21.4.4 Access Resources

Once approved, access the resources and tools available to nonprofits through the Google for Nonprofits program.

21.5 Conclusion

Google for Nonprofits is a valuable program that offers nonprofits access to a range of resources and tools to help them achieve their mission. By taking advantage of these resources, nonprofits can increase their online presence, engage with their audience, and drive donations. To get started with Google for Nonprofits, check eligibility, apply, wait for approval, and access resources.

TL : DR

Google for Nonprofits is a program that offers eligible nonprofits access to a range of free and discounted Google products and services to increase their online presence, engage with their audience, and drive donations. The program offers resources such as Google Ad Grants, Google Workspace, YouTube Nonprofit Program, Google One Today, and Google Earth Outreach. To get started, nonprofits should check eligibility, apply, wait for approval, and access resources.

NOTES